# Have A Happy...

MILDRED PITTS WALTER has won numerous awards for her work, including the Coretta Scott King Award and the Parents' Choice Award. She lives in Denver, Colorado.

# Have A Happy...

## Mildred Pitts Walter

### Illustrated by Carole Byard

**HARCOURT BRACE & COMPANY**
Orlando   Atlanta   Austin   Boston   San Francisco   Chicago   Dallas   New York
Toronto   London

## ACKNOWLEDGMENTS

The information used in the chapters about Kwanzaa, the Kwanzaa symbols, principles, and ritual, is from the work by Dr. Mauiana Karenga, *Kwanzaa: Origin, Concepts, Practice* (Los Angeles: Kawaida Publications, 1977).

Thanks to Dr. Akbarali Thobhani, Director of the Institute for Intercultural Studies, Metropolitan State College, Denver, and to the Hue-Man Experience Book Store of Denver for their assistance.

Printed in the United States of America

ISBN 0-15-300348-0

14  15   059   02

*For Isetta and Opalonga,*
*who keep alive the idea of Kwanzaa.*

# ONE

The long Christmas holiday had finally begun. Christopher, carrying gifts he had made for his family, walked hurriedly out of the school yard. Miles and Jamal raced by on their bicycles. Chris braced himself against the cold blasts of wind. He wished he had a bike, too.

He clasped the packages to his body and pulled his cap farther down over his ears. Several of his fingers were pushing through his well-worn gloves, and he blew on them to get them warm. Hurrying, he turned backward against the wind.

As he neared Miles's house, he saw that Jamal's bicycle was parked next to Miles's bike. The garage door opened and Miles called out, "Hey, Chris, come help me fold my papers."

"I've got to pick up my sister," Chris answered.

1

"Come on, Chris," Miles pleaded. "Just for a little while. I'll give you thirty-five cents."

"How much you giving *me*?" Jamal asked.

"Nothing," Miles answered. "You got more money than me."

*Thirty-five cents*, Chris thought, *that's a lot*. But he said, "I can't."

"Fifty cents."

"Okay." Then, not wanting them to know just how much he needed the fifty cents, he said, "I'll come for a little while, but I won't charge you."

In the closed garage, they folded and put rubber bands on newspapers that Miles would deliver that afternoon.

"What you getting for Christmas?" Jamal asked.

Miles answered first. "I don't think I'm getting much. I just got a lotta stuff for my birthday. This new bike, even. But I'll get something, what you bet?"

Chris kept on working as if he had not heard the question. He didn't want to talk about presents. His daddy hadn't worked steadily in eighteen months. His mama had said that this year Christmas might be like any other day for them.

Jamal went on, "My daddy sent my gifts already. Something big, but I don't know what."

"What I really want," Miles put in, "is a seat bag for my bike."

"Get one like mine," Jamal said. "Mine can hold my lunch, tire tubes, and tools. It's neat, man. Only cost about twenty bucks."

"Did your daddy send you that from Cleveland?" Chris asked without looking up.

**2**

"For my birthday," Jamal answered.

Chris remembered Jamal's birthday. *No party for me, ever. Everybody's too busy.*

They worked with only the crackling of paper and click of rubber bands. Finally Miles asked, "What you getting for Christmas, Chris?"

"I don't know." The answer came quickly.

"What you mean, don't know? What you want, man?" Jamal asked.

"Nothing for Christmas..."

"Nothing!" Miles interrupted.

"I want a bike for my birthday."

"Oh, that's right. You were born on Christmas Day. Christopher Noel Dodd. I always forget."

"That's all right. *Every*body forgets," Chris said sadly. "But I'll be eleven years old, just like you guys, this Christmas Day."

"It's uncool being born on Christmas Day," Jamal said, and laughed.

"Yeah, nothing cool about it at all." Chris didn't laugh. "Every present is a Christmas *and* birthday present."

All the papers folded, they began stuffing them into the double basket on the back of Miles's bike. Chris admired the sleek lines of the bicycle. Suddenly he thought about the time. "I forgot. I gotta go. Uncle Ronald is probably at my house right now. I'm making stuff for his Kwanzaa celebration."

"His what?" Jamal asked.

"Kwanzaa," Miles answered. "Don't you know what Kwanzaa is?"

"Never heard of it. What is it?"

"A celebration for us Black people," Miles said.

**4**

"Aw, man. That ain't telling me what it means."

"*Kwanzaa* means first fruit harvest," Chris said.

"Like Thanksgiving?"

"No-oo, no. Not like that," Chris replied.

"Then what is it?" Jamal persisted.

"It's a celebration. I gotta go." Chris grabbed his packages and started out.

"Hey, man, your money." Miles ran after him.

"No. It's okay." Chris waved him off. He still didn't want his friends to know he needed the fifty cents.

"But I promised. Here, and have a merry Christmas." Miles pressed the money into his hand.

"Don't wish me a merry Christmas. Wish me a happy birthday."

"I will—on your birthday."

Chris put the two quarters in his pocket and remembered the time when money hadn't seemed that important. He carried his gifts carefully, not wanting to crush the colorful wrappings. Everyone else in his fifth-grade class had made only one gift. But Mrs. Rush, his teacher, had let him make three: a towel rack for his mama, a tie rack for his daddy, and a small dollhouse for Beth, his five-year-old sister. Creating things with his hands was what he liked best.

The sun lowered, the wind blew colder. Chris hurried toward home. Trunks of tall trees wrapped with silver, red, and green foil made the walk a shiny lane. He passed brightly decorated houses. One had a Santa in a sleigh pulled by only one prancing reindeer. Chris knew that as soon as night fell his street would glow with lights, gold and white and all the colors of the rainbow.

5

In other years, a tree had stood in their big window, too, glittering a colorful greeting. *Maybe we won't be getting a Christmas tree*, he thought. *Probably not, with Daddy spending money looking for a job.* His daddy had been out of town a whole week trying to find work.

But it was not the tree that was troubling Chris. The haunting unhappiness that he often felt at this season came over him now. *December twenty-fifth should be my day, the way December third is Miles's and June twenty-eighth is Jamal's. But no, it's always merry Christmas, Chris!*

Chris knew he should have picked up Beth long ago. Remembering his uncle, he walked faster.

He didn't want Beth to see the gifts, so he went by home first. His uncle had not come. He quickly hid his packages in his room and ran to the babysitter's house.

Beth stood holding her wrapped packages, looking out the window, waiting impatiently. "You late," she scolded.

"How you know I'm late? You can't even tell time." Chris let the sitter know they were leaving. As they started home, he asked, "What's all that you got?"

"Presents I made."

"What'd you make?"

"It's a secret."

"Bet I can guess," Chris teased.

"Bet you can't."

"Let me hold them."

Reluctantly she handed him the packages. One felt thin as paper. The other, though smaller, felt heavy.

**6**

"I know I can guess," he said, "but I'll give you another chance to tell me."

"The little one is my hand for Daddy. The other is my picture for Mama."

"I knew all along that's what it was," Chris said smugly.

"You didn't."

Sensing she knew she had been tricked into telling, he dodged out of reach as she tried to shove him off the walk and escaped, laughing. "Every kindergartner makes a clay handprint and a paper silhouette for Christmas." The sad look on her face made him quickly add, "Mama and Daddy'll like them."

"How you know?"

"They liked mine. They still have them."

The house was cold and no aroma of good things cooking welcomed them. Before, when their daddy had a job, their mama was often home when they came in from school. A nurse, she had worked part-time. Now, not only was she on the job full-time, she often stayed overtime.

Chris turned on the heat. Then he went into the kitchen with Beth following. He looked into the refrigerator but found nothing tempting. "You hungry?"

"No," Beth answered. "I had some toast and milk. When is Daddy coming home?"

"Maybe Sunday." With their jackets still on, they sat in the kitchen, not talking.

# TWO

Hey, what's going on here?" Uncle Ronald walked into the kitchen loaded down with groceries. "You guys going someplace?"

"Hi, Uncle Ronald," Beth cried, happy to see him.

"Why you ask if we going someplace?" Chris wanted to know.

"You have your jackets on. Where's that sister of mine?"

"Mama hasn't come yet. She's late," Chris replied.

"Well, how about some help here, putting this stuff away?"

They scrambled out of their jackets and looked into the bags. "Is this fried chicken for us, too?" Beth asked.

"If you let me stay and have supper with you."

Beth set the table while Chris helped to slice the carrots, cucumbers, and celery his uncle had

9

brought. When they took the chicken out of the box they discovered four biscuits with honey.

"How can we divide four biscuits among three people?" Uncle Ronald wanted to know.

"Give me two and you guys have one," Chris said.

"No, give me the two," Beth shouted.

"Wait, wait, just a minute. I think the person with the longest legs should decide," Uncle Ronald said.

Just then Mama came home.

"Mama, Mama," Beth shrieked. "Give it to Mama."

"I'll take it, whatever it is," Mama said, and they all laughed. Chris felt glad that she had come home.

After dinner, Uncle Ronald handed Chris a package. "Here's that stuff you asked me to get so you can finish up my animals."

In the package Chris found glue, some wood, and several packages of clothespins. "Want to see what I've done already?" he asked his uncle.

"Yeah, I'll come in a minute."

Chris went to his room and lined up all the finished animals. On smooth wood he had drawn ducks, rabbits, a mouse, reindeer, pigs, and birds. He had clamped the wood onto his workbench, then cut the animals out with his coping saw. His dad had given him a wood burner. With that he had made mouths, noses, ears, and eyes, and on some animals he had burned special designs.

Chris was excited about the job he had done. He hoped his uncle would like the animals, too. He waited impatiently, but Uncle Ronald didn't come. Finally he decided to return to the kitchen. He found

Mama and Uncle Ronald huddled together, whispering.

"Are you coming?" Chris demanded.

"Christopher!" His mama called him that when she was not pleased with him. "You know better than to interrupt without saying excuse me."

"I'm coming, man." Uncle Ronald gave Chris a smile.

Back in his room, Chris wondered what they were whispering about. Had something happened to Daddy? Maybe he wasn't coming back at all, ever. *Surely Mama would tell me if that was so.*

Soon Uncle Ronald came bursting into the room. Chris was always amazed at how young his uncle looked and acted, for a high school teacher. Maybe it was because he was not a big, tall man. But to Chris he seemed to fill a room.

"Wow! These are great!" Uncle Ronald's pleasure warmed Chris. He picked up the animals and turned them about. "Let's see, now," he went on. "You have ten. Can you make ten more by Monday?"

"Why that many?" Chris asked.

"I need them for Kwanzaa, man."

"My daddy's coming Sunday. Monday's Christmas Eve. I might have something else to do."

"You can make them. Give it a try, anyway."

Still curious about the whispering he had heard in the kitchen, Chris said, "Uncle Ronald..." Then, remembering being embarrassed by his mama, he hesitated. "Oh, never mind."

"What is it, man?"

The way his uncle said "man" always put Chris at ease.

11

"What were you and Mama talking about?"

Uncle Ronald laughed. "That's between me and my sister." He was the youngest of four: two sisters and two brothers. Chris's mama was next to him, two years older. Uncle Ronald was already thirty.

*He laughed. Couldn't be something bad. Then why can't they include me in the secret?* Chris felt hurt.

His uncle was about to leave, but Chris wanted him to stay longer. "Uncle Ronald, what is Kwanzaa besides a celebration?"

"Isn't that enough?" Uncle Ronald asked, and laughed.

"Well, my friend Jamal wanted to know if it's like Thanksgiving."

"In a way, yes. *Kwanzaa* is taken from the African Swahili word *kwanza*, spelled with one *a*, which means 'first.' It is part of the phrase *matunda ya kwanza*, which means 'first fruit.' When I was in the Peace Corps in Ghana, I went to a celebration called *kwanza* for the harvest of the first fruit. That African celebration is somewhat like our Thanksgiving."

"Then what is our Kwanzaa?"

"Our Kwanzaa is spelled with two *a*'s but is pronounced the same. It is an African-American word. Now, know how we like to get together? Well, Kwanzaa is a get-together, or an ingathering, with a special purpose."

"Oh, I see. Like when we talk about the past and ancestors at the celebration. And when Grandma Ida and other older people talk about remembering, and stuff like that, huh?"

"Yes. Exactly. We celebrate ourselves as a people."

12

"Uncle Ronald, were you and Mama talking about Daddy?" Chris was still worried.

"Oh, no. Nothing like that." He drew Chris to him. "I can't tell you, but I promise, it's nothing to make you unhappy." He picked up a package of clothespins and asked, "Why did you have me buy these?"

"I can't tell you, but I promise it won't make you unhappy."

Uncle Ronald touched Chris's chin lightly with his fist, and they both laughed.

After saying goodbye to his uncle, Chris found Mama in the kitchen with Beth.

"Your sister said you were late today," Mama said sharply.

"I wasn't. Not *that* late." He glared at Beth, who stared at him wide-eyed. "Why'd you have to tell?" he snapped at her.

"You kept me waiting. A long time." Beth lowered her eyes.

"What happened, Chris?" Mama wanted to know.

"Mama, I helped Miles fold his papers. She doesn't know what late is."

"I depend on you to get home on time," Mama said.

"I do get home on time." He looked at Beth with a scowl.

"Mama, when will we get our Christmas tree?" Beth asked.

"I don't know," Mama said impatiently.

*What's the matter with her*, Chris wondered. He felt a lump rising in his throat. His mama was never like this before. He was sure there would be nothing for his birthday or Christmas. Suddenly he felt angry. "I don't care if we don't have a tree," he said.

**13**

"What's wrong with you, Chris?" Mama asked.

"Nothing. I just don't want a tree. I want a bicycle for my birthday."

"Let Santa bring you a bicycle. He brings things, huh, Mama?" Beth put in.

"Santa doesn't bring birthday presents," Chris retorted.

They were quiet. The silence was uncomfortable. Chris was glad when Beth said, "Well, Mama. Are we? Gonna get a tree?"

"Beth, we'll have to wait until your daddy comes."

"Is he still coming Sunday?" Chris wanted to know.

"Yes."

Chris sensed Mama's bad mood, but he asked anyway. "What were you and Uncle Ronald whispering about, Mama?"

She gave a little laugh. "None of your business."

The laugh encouraged him. "Aw, Mama, you can tell me."

"I can, but I won't."

"Will you tell me why we can't get our tree tomorrow?" Beth persisted.

"I have to work, for one thing." She picked up their jackets, which they had thrown over the kitchen stool.

"But tomorrow is Saturday," Chris blurted out. "When we going shopping?"

"There's no money for shopping. And I know tomorrow is Saturday, and I have to work. You can go over to your grandma's and help keep Beth."

"No, I can't." He shifted his weight and looked at

**14**

Mama. She looked so tired and sad, he softened. "Do I have to?"

"Is there any good reason why you can't?"

"It's just that I have all those things to make for Uncle Ronald. I promised."

"Let me go to Grandma Ida's by myself," Beth pleaded.

"Your grandma might be busy tomorrow, and I don't want Chris here alone." Mama handed Beth the jackets. "Put these away, please."

Chris went to his room feeling angry and ashamed. Ashamed that he did not want to help take care of Beth. *But why can't she take off just one day?* As he worked, burning wings on birds, lines for a mouse's ear, and fat wrinkles on a pig, he wondered why he couldn't stay home alone. *Wish Daddy was here.*

# THREE

Chris woke to the sound of laughter. *That could only be Grandma*, he thought. He bounded out of bed and dressed hurriedly. Maybe Grandma Ida would talk Mama into letting him stay home.

Mama had her coat on ready to leave for work. Grandma was at the kitchen counter dipping slices of bread into egg batter. Chris smiled and said a warm good morning.

"Come here and give me a hug," Grandma said, beaming.

Chris knew that was coming and wished she would learn that he was too big for that now. He shyly hesitated.

"C'mon," she said. "You never outgrow hugs, boy." She grabbed him.

He felt a flush of warmth around his head. He

**17**

quickly hugged her back and escaped. Without looking at her he asked, "What you making?"

"Your favorite—French toast, and I brought over some sausages," his grandmother announced.

"Mama, why can't I stay home today?" Chris asked.

"Because I don't like you being here by yourself."

"But I'll be all right," Chris pleaded.

"I don't know that," Mama said.

"I won't let *anybody* in. I'll just do my work."

"I still don't like leaving you."

"Aw, Mama," Chris complained. "I'd be all right, huh, Grandma?"

"I don't see why not. Just this once," Grandma said.

"Well, all right. But I'm going to let Mr. Charles know you here and to keep an eye out. If you need anything, you call him."

Chris liked the next-door neighbors and was glad they were there if he needed them.

"Now listen," Mama said. "Let me find this house in one piece when I get back, you hear? And don't you go anyplace until I come home."

"Aw, Mama. I'm no baby."

"Oh, no?" Mama laughed. "That's news. Get Beth up. I gotta run. Be good, now, and remember what I told you. I have enough to worry about."

As he left the room, he heard his grandma say, "Myra, you should trust him. He's a good child."

When Grandma Ida and Beth finally left, the quiet in the house overwhelmed Chris. Feeling a little scared, he circled through the house, checking to see if all the doors were locked. In the living room, surrounded by familiar things, he felt big, proud to be alone. Then he went to his room, glad he had a lot of work to do.

Unwrapping a package of clothespins, he thought about the little chair, the bed, and the dresser he planned to make for Beth's dollhouse. He had seen his daddy make beautiful things with clothespins. Now he would try to make some furniture with them.

Chris discovered that the spring wires in clothespins come out more easily than they go in. As he removed them, he had an idea. Clothespins would make animals, too. He glued together legs, bodies, and other parts to make a giraffe, a horse, and a reindeer.

All morning he worked on the animals, remembering all the things his daddy had taught him. When he finished the giraffe, Chris was so pleased he wanted to run out and show it to somebody, just anybody, and say, "Look, *I* made this!" Instead he kept on working.

By the time he had finished three animals and started on the chair for Beth's dollhouse, he was hungry. He hurriedly stuffed down peanut butter and jelly sandwiches and leftover French toast, then went back to work on the chair.

Carefully he turned the pins so the indentations for the spring wires made interesting lines. He mixed and matched the varying shades of wood to make contrasts. When all the parts were glued, he had a real rocking chair.

He looked at it. Something was missing.

**19**

He figured out what to do. He took four pieces from two pins and placed them with the thinner part at the bottom, so the space that held the wire faced the back of the chair. He spread them to look like a Chinese fan, then glued them together. When the glue dried, he stuck them onto the back of the chair. It looked like a granny rocking chair. *Ah, my best piece ever.*

Now he was ready to make the bed. He looked around. Oh no, only one clothespin left. How could he make the bed and dresser for Beth's house? He tried to cut something from a piece of wood. That didn't work. Then he thought, *Toothpicks!*

In the kitchen he found two kinds: round thick picks and flat thin ones. *These will make a good bed and dresser,* he said to himself.

He had just finished them when the doorbell rang. *Who could that be?* he wondered. His first thought was not to answer. But maybe it was his neighbor.

At the door he heard Miles's voice. Should he open the door? When he opened it, he found Jamal there, too. They were on their bikes.

"We're going to the Toy-orama exhibit," said Miles. "Wanta come?"

"Can't."

"Ask your mama," Jamal said.

"My mama's working."

"Then come on, man," Jamal demanded.

He didn't want Jamal to think he was a baby. "How long you gonna be gone?"

"Not long," Miles said. "With us on our bikes, if

you ride your skateboard, we'll be there in no time."

There wasn't much more work to do. He had finished the furniture and three animals. Maybe he could go. Chris rushed to his room to get his jacket. Then his grandmother's words rang in his mind: *Myra, you should trust him.*

He went back to the door. "I better not."

"Aw, come on." Miles acted disappointed.

"Yeah, man," Jamal pleaded.

"I can't, really. I'm still working on that stuff for Kwanzaa."

"Oh, yeah. Your uncle wants us to come over on Christmas Day for that."

"Aw, shut up, silly," Miles said, punching Jamal on the shoulder. "Kwanzaa's not on Christmas Day. It starts the day after."

"Oh, so you saw Uncle Ronald," Chris said, pleased.

"Yeah. I still don't understand what Kwanzaa's all about," Jamal complained.

*If I tell him all about it, he might not come.* "You'll have to see it. It's something you show, not tell," Chris said.

Finally they left. Chris went back to his work. He smiled. *So Uncle Ronald invited them to Kwanzaa. Silly Jamal, thinking it's on Christmas Day.* He thought about his daddy. *Be home tomorrow.* His heart leaped. *Maybe he got a job and I can have a bike for my birthday.*

By the time Mama came home, he had finished three clothespin animals and drawn seven more to

**22**

make the ten Uncle Ronald wanted. He only had to cut them out. For that he had another whole day plus some. The house was all in one piece, and he had kept his promise.

# FOUR

<hr />

Sunday crawled along. After church and lunch at his grandma's house, Chris came home to work. But nothing went right. His mind was not on making animals. Finally, he gave up and lay on his bed thinking about Daddy coming home. *If only we could afford plane fare. He'd be home by now. A plane goes much faster than the bus. What if he missed the bus?* Chris didn't want to think about that.

The drawings of the seven animals lay on the board waiting. He got up and started working with his coping saw. After cutting only two, still bored, he went to find Mama and Beth. The house creaked in the quiet as he peeped in on Beth, fast asleep in her room. Mama, in the den with the TV on, was fast asleep, too. *How can they sleep when Daddy's coming home?*

He looked at the clock in the kitchen. Only three

o'clock. He wished it were five. Then he wouldn't have to wait any longer. There was food, but he wasn't hungry. He felt full all the way up into his throat.

Back in his room he cut out three more animals. Only two more to go. He decided to put faces on the finished ones. He messed up two, one after the other. Disgusted, he fell on his bed.

A gentle shake and Mama's quiet voice awoke him. "Daddy's home."

At first he thought he was still asleep. He kept his eyes closed.

"Chris," his father said.

Chris sprang up. The look on Daddy's face was one of joy, yet Chris saw something else. Worry. Something almost like fear. Chris knew he hadn't gotten a job. He clung to Daddy's waist and buried his face in his father's firm stomach. With his eyes closed tight he hung on until the unshed tears passed away. Finally the words came. "I'm glad you home."

Later that evening, Beth asked if they could have a tree. "I think we can have a tree. What's Christmas without a tree?" Daddy said.

"See, Chris," Beth said. "He didn't want a tree, Daddy."

"You don't want a tree, Chris?" Daddy asked.

"Oh, she's just a tattletale. I said I'd rather have a birthday present."

"Beth, Chris, it's time for you guys to go to bed," Mama said.

"Since when do I have to go to bed when she goes?" Chris asked.

"Let Chris stay. He's old enough to know what we're up against."

After Beth was tucked in, his father talked about going to several towns, only to find there was no work. Many people were looking for jobs.

Chris knew Daddy had worked as an electronics assembler. He was part of a group that put together circuit boards for computer hardware. The company he worked for went out of business, leaving hundreds of people out of work. Now, as his father talked, Chris realized that eighteen months was almost two years. *That's a long time*, he thought.

"We might have to move out of this area," Daddy said. His voice had a strange sound.

*Move.* What would Chris do if he had to leave Grandma Ida, Uncle Ronald, all of his friends?

"I hope it won't come to that," Mama said.

"Hey, son." Daddy's voice startled Chris out of his thoughts. "I haven't forgotten. You want a bike for Christmas."

"No, for my birthday," Chris said.

"Oh, you make it tough for me." Daddy laughed. "If you wanted it for Christmas, I could easily say Santa can't come this year."

Mama said, "Yes, Chris knows Santa doesn't bring birthday presents."

"I don't see how we can manage a bike this year, Chris." His father did not look up.

"But Daddy, I need it. I'd like to deliver papers."

"Now, Chris . . ."

Before Mama could finish, Daddy said, "I'm glad you want to do that. Maybe, just maybe now, we can work something out."

**27**

"There's no sense in raising his hopes, Bruce," Mama said. "He needs other things more than he needs a bike. Shoes, for instance. He has to think of more than what he *wants*."

Chris wished Mama would see that he *was* thinking of more than just what he wanted. He could deliver papers and help out, too. He sat there hoping Daddy would say something to make her understand. But there was only silence between them.

Finally Daddy said, "How's your project for Ronald coming?"

"Want to see?"

In Chris's room, Daddy's face brightened. "You finished all of those while I was away? You're getting good. I better watch you. You'll outdo me, man."

Chris, pleased, showed him everything he had made except Beth's furniture. That had to remain a secret.

His father became serious. "Chris, your mama wants you to have a bike as much as I, but she's worried." He took Chris's chin in his hand and lifted Chris's face up toward his. "I don't want you to worry, though. We've had some good times in this house, haven't we?" His voice sounded as though he was about to cry.

Chris looked away. "Yes."

"We'll have good times again." Now Daddy sounded like himself. "Look at me, Chris. That I promise you." He pulled Chris to him briefly, then went back to the kitchen.

Alone, Chris sat on his bed thinking about this time last year. Even though his father had been out

28

of work for six months, there had been hope. They'd all had a good time then.

He looked over into the corner of his room where last year's Christmas present, a train with a shiny black engine and silver, blue-streaked cars, stood on the track. He remembered how he and his daddy had put it all together. They had mounted the tracks on a board and built a tunnel and a small station.

*We* have *had good times*, he thought. He wanted to believe his father when he said they would have them again. But Chris was afraid.

Chris woke up in an unusually quiet house. There were no signs or sounds that today was the day before Christmas, the day before his birthday. *Where is everybody?* he wondered on his way to the kitchen.

Daddy was sitting at the table with his cup half full of coffee, looking at the want ads section of the newspaper. Chris knew from the burned bits of toast on the plate that his daddy had made breakfast. "Where's Mama?" he asked.

"She's working today."

"We not going shopping today?"

"We're going for a Christmas tree," Daddy answered.

"Is that all?" Disappointment sounded in Chris's voice. Mama had never worked on Christmas Eve before. Daddy was always home by noon on that day, and the family did special things together: last-minute shopping, visiting family and friends, and cooking special foods for Christmas Day.

"That's all the shopping." Daddy, annoyed, returned to his paper.

**29**

Chris felt closed out. Maybe he had asked the wrong question. Finally he said, "What's for breakfast?"

"Why don't I make you some hot cereal and cinnamon toast?"

Knowing his daddy's toast, Chris shook his head. "You make the cereal. I'll make the toast."

"That's a deal. Get Beth up."

While they had breakfast, the phone rang. "I'll get it," Chris said. It was Uncle Ronald.

"How you coming along, man?" Uncle Ronald wanted to know. "Can I pick up my stuff today?"

Chris tried to show some enthusiasm. "They're coming. I'll have them done."

The day went too fast for Chris. He worked hard, but he made mistakes. At almost five o'clock he was still trying to perfect animals. Beth was impatient to go for the Christmas tree, and kept bothering him. Finally he shouted, "Go on. I don't have to go."

"Daddy says you have to. So hurry up."

# FIVE

**D**arkness had set in early. As they rode across town, Chris noticed people in hats and scarves loaded down with packages. *Why can't we be out shopping? No, we don't get anything this year.* He sank down in the seat, wishing he hadn't come.

Finally they came to the place near the railway yard where there were lots of Christmas trees. Some men were beginning to put them into boxcars to haul them away.

"You came just in time," one of the men said. "Business was terrible this year. We didn't sell many trees, so take your pick. Take two or three." He laughed.

Beth wanted a tree with heavy bushy branches. Chris found a tall silver-tip fir. Its cone shape was almost perfect. The branches formed circles. All of a sudden he realized he did want a Christmas tree

31

after all. "This is it, Daddy," Chris called excitedly.

"Chris, you *would* choose that one. It's probably the most expensive tree on the lot."

"I got fifty cents," Chris said.

"That won't buy one branch of that tree," Daddy said.

"Aw, Daddy, let's ask."

They took it to the man directing the loading of the trees. "Make me an offer," the man said.

"Fifty cents," Chris answered eagerly.

"You don't really want *that* tree, do you?" the man said.

"Oh, yes we do." Beth spoke before Daddy or Chris had a chance.

"All right. You can have it for that."

Chris gave the man the fifty cents, glad now that Miles had insisted on paying him.

"Have a merry Christmas," the man said.

Chris and Beth shouted thanks and merry Christmas as they drove out of the lot.

As soon as they pulled into their driveway, Mama rushed outside. Without even noticing the tree, she called excitedly, "Come see, come on!"

They all rushed into the kitchen. Food covered the table and counter. There was a big turkey and a ham. Greens, sweet potatoes, yams, all kinds of fruits and vegetables, and many, many cans of food were spread about.

"Wow! Where'd all that come from, Mama?" Chris shouted. He glanced at Daddy, feeling how lucky they were. But what was that look on Daddy's face? Chris did not understand. Was his father feeling ashamed? Was he going to cry?

32

Then Daddy grinned. "Can't beat neighbors like ours," he said. "No, can't beat this with a switch."

"Now, Mama," Chris said, "you come see what we got."

Mama took one look and put her hand up to her face. "Oh," she said to Daddy, "why did you let them talk you into buying that tree? We can't afford a silver-tip."

Chris wanted to explain, but Beth, excited, took over and told what had happened. "And it didn't cost but fifty cents, huh, Daddy?"

"And our son paid for it." Daddy put a hand on Chris's shoulder.

"It's beautiful," Mama said. "That tree needs no decorations."

"Oh, yes it does. I'll get them," Beth said and ran inside with Chris right behind her. She rushed to the closet where year after year decorations were stored away until the next Christmas.

"Wait, Beth," Chris demanded. But Beth pulled at the nearest box, and all the boxes came tumbling down. Lights and silver, blue, green, and red balls splattered over the floor. Many were in slivers.

"Beth!" Chris screamed. "Look what you've done!"

Mama and Daddy rushed into the room. "What's going on in here?" Mama asked, irritated.

Chris saw Beth's face scrunch up to cry, but he didn't care. "Miss Fast here has broken all the decorations," he said angrily.

"That's no reason for you to shout at her," Mama snapped at Chris.

"Don't get on me," Chris shouted back. "Get on Beth. She's the one. Now we have no decorations."

"All right!" Daddy exclaimed. "Stop this shouting, all of you. You don't talk to your mother and sister like that, Chris."

"What's wrong with him?" Mama asked. "He's been beside himself here lately."

"Now you apologize or go to your room," Daddy said.

Chris looked at his father. *I didn't do anything. Beth did. Mama screamed at me. Why do I have to apologize?* He folded his arms, brought them down hard on his chest. "I'm sorry," he muttered and ran to his room.

The animals were gone. Uncle Ronald must have come and taken them away. His room seemed empty now without them. Still smoldering, he wished his Uncle Ronald would take him, too.

He heard voices outside and knew his family was decorating the tree. *With what?* he wondered. He wanted to forget his anger and go help. *After all, it's my tree. I bought it.* But instead of helping, he stayed in his room, feeling worried. *Something is happening. We weren't like this before. Shouting at me and going on. Daddy better get a job.*

At bedtime he got under the covers and lay there trying hard to stay awake until the house became quiet. He wanted to see the tree and be the last person to put gifts under it. And he wanted to see if, just maybe, he might find a bicycle there.

He sang softly to himself. He recited nursery rhymes and counted backward from a hundred three times. Then he listened to see just how many sounds there were in the night. Dogs barked. Car horns honked and a lone siren screamed in the distance.

The hum of the city reminded him of the sound in a seashell.

He dozed. Then he woke with a start and lay listening. All was still. He said a prayer for a bike and quietly got out of bed. He took his packages from their hiding place and, tiptoeing, made his way toward the living room.

Excitedly he looked all around the room. By the light that came in from outside, he could see that there was no bicycle. The tree stood in the window like one in a forest, blanketed with snow. The spotlight under it, covered with a blue sheet of cellophane, was now off. Beth's packages were there, the lighter one hanging from a branch. There were other packages, too. In the semidarkness he lifted them and felt their weight.

He turned on the spotlight. What was it that looked so much like glistening snow? The blue light on the snow gave it a cold feeling. The tree looks so alone, he thought. Suddenly Chris, too, felt alone and lonely.

# SIX

Chris slept late the next morning. His family was up and about when Beth, already dressed, burst into his room.

"Get up, Chris. We wanta open our presents," she said.

Chris lay there, hating to move.

"Come on," Beth pleaded. "Get up. We gonna open them without you."

"I don't care, go on."

"Chris, come on," Mama called. "We're waiting for you."

Reluctantly he got up. When he walked into the living room, Beth, impatient, had already begun to open her presents. She liked her dollhouse, and when she opened the package with the furniture, she let out a squeal of joy. The chair was too big to go

**37**

through the door or window, but the toothpick bed and dresser were just right.

"How'd you make this snow, Mama?" Chris wanted to know.

"That's a big secret," Mama said jokingly.

"She made it with hot water and soap flakes," Beth said. "She put it in the mixer, and me and Daddy plopped it on the branches with our hands."

"Looks real," Chris said. He opened presents to find shoes from Mama, a sweater from Grandma Ida, and a pair of gloves from Daddy. He tried to appear excited, but he felt disappointed.

Beth handed him her present. It was light like paper. Chris, excited now, opened it. Beth had drawn a big Santa saying, "Merry Christmas to my brother, Chris." He sighed. *Just another Christmas card. Why can't people take my birthday seriously? They could just say, Have a happy. Then I could add anything I want: happy birthday, happy Christmas, happy Kwanzaa, happy New Year....* Then he looked at Beth with a weak smile. "You made this. Thanks."

He began to feel better when Mama and Daddy made a big fuss over the things he had made for them and Beth. The chair was just the right size for Beth's small doll. Chris found some soft wire. He quickly made a pair of eyeglasses and put them on the doll. She became a granny for the rocking chair.

"Now, Chris," Mama said, "hurry up and get dressed. Ronald invited us over."

Chris played around, moving the furniture in and out of Beth's dollhouse and adjusting the doll's eyeglasses to make them fit better. He was not interested in getting dressed or in going anywhere. *What's*

*the use*, he thought. It would be the same all day, nobody noticing that he had turned eleven.

"Chris, get up, right now, and get dressed," Mama demanded. "Put on something nice."

Reluctantly, he went to his room, taking his time even though he knew they were ready, waiting for him. *Why do we have to go to Uncle Ronald's so early?* He snatched socks out of his drawer. "Do I have to get dressed up?" he shouted.

"It's Christmas and your birthday, Chris. You should want to look nice," Mama called.

Finally, they were on their way. Chris sat in the backseat with Beth, frozen inside with unhappiness.

The blinds on his uncle's windows were closed when they arrived. "Looks like Uncle Ronald isn't even at home," Chris said sullenly.

"Well, he invited us," Mama said.

"Go ring the doorbell and see, Chris," his father suggested.

Chris unwillingly got out of the car, thinking of his warm bed. He leaned on the doorbell. The door opened and he was pulled inside. The sudden bedlam frightened Chris. Horns blew, floating streamers of paper wrapped around him. Lots of people shouted, "Happy birthday, Chris! Happy birthday!"

Overwhelmed, Chris could not move. He could not speak. He didn't know what to do.

Miles and Jamal were there looking at him, smiling. All of his family: uncles, aunts, cousins, and Grandma Ida. Everybody. Mama, Daddy, and Beth finally came in. Still he couldn't say a word.

Uncle Ronald said, "Here is the birthday boy at last. So, say something, Chris."

**40**

Chris tried to think of something to say. He looked at all of his friends. Only one thing came into his mind. "Have a happy . . . no, merry Christmas!"

After everyone had had their fill of small sandwiches, birthday cake, and ice cream, Uncle Ronald called for their attention. "First, let me invite all of you back here tomorrow for the Kwanzaa celebration. Tomorrow, December twenty-sixth, is the first day."

Then he looked at Chris and smiled. "Chris is now eleven, middle-aged." Everybody laughed. Uncle Ronald went on, "Today is Chris's day. So on *his* day, it is his turn to be important. And what does an important person do?" He paused. "What do you think, Chris?"

Chris glanced toward the table at gifts that weren't wrapped in Christmas paper. "Get presents?" he answered cautiously. He was unable to hide his excitement. *Maybe now I'll get that bicycle*, he thought.

"Have you thought that sometimes important people *give* gifts?" his uncle asked.

"But that's *very* important people," Chris said. There was soft laughter.

"Well, that's exactly what you're going to be today. A very important person. You're going to give gifts." His uncle brought out packages wrapped in colorful paper.

Chris gave everyone a package, thinking, *I must be jinxed. Whoever heard of the birthday person giving gifts?*

"Oo-ooo-o, look at this," Grandma Ida said. "A giraffe!"

"Chris made those with his own hands!" Uncle Ronald exclaimed.

"I don't believe you made this," Jamal said happily. He had one of the animals made of clothespins.

"He made them. Chris makes real nice things," Miles said.

Chris listened to their praises, and satisfaction warmed him.

"Now," Uncle Ronald said, "here are your presents, Chris." He led Chris to the table.

Right then, Chris knew there would be no bicycle. He opened his presents: a game from Jamal, puzzles from Miles. Uncle Ronald gave him blades for his coping saw. He also received paints and paintbrushes. His excitement showed when he thanked everyone.

As Miles and Jamal were leaving, Jamal asked, "Did you get a bicycle?"

Chris's face felt hot, but before he could answer, Miles said, "His birthday isn't over yet."

When everyone had left, Chris said to Uncle Ronald, "So that's what all the whispering was about, huh? And ten more animals for Kwanzaa!"

His uncle grinned. Chris knew this was the happiest day of his life and the best birthday he had ever had. But he was not so sure that giving was better than getting gifts. He still longed for a bike.

# SEVEN

The day after his birthday, Chris's parents asked him to stay home just in case his daddy had to go out. Daddy did have to go out, and now Chris sat in his room waiting for Beth to wake up from her nap. He'd gotten tired of her chattering and had told her if she didn't go to sleep, she couldn't go to Kwanzaa. The first celebration started at six that evening. Only three hours away. Bored, he checked the wheel bearings on his skateboard. The wheels turned fast and smoothly. He took care of his board, his means of getting around. But it wasn't a bicycle.

*Bet my friends are all out now. Riding.* Any other holiday he'd be with them, Mama at home taking care of Beth.

He wandered into the kitchen, wishing Daddy would come home. *Maybe he got a job.* His heart beat faster. *Probably not.* He sank into a chair.

**43**

Beth found him with his head down on the table. "Chris, what's the matter?"

He started up. "Nothing."

She sat at the table looking at him. "You worried?" she asked.

"Why should I be worried?" he answered, annoyed.

"Because we here by ourselves," she said.

"Naw." But he did feel worried. Frightened about a lot of things that he didn't understand. Couldn't talk about. He felt that lump rising in his throat.

"Well, you worried about something else?" she persisted.

"Why you asking all these questions?"

"*I'm* worried," she said, and started to cry. "I want Mama to come home."

"She'll be here," he said, trying to make Beth feel better. "It's already three o'clock."

Just then Daddy walked into the kitchen. "Did you get a job?" Chris asked before Daddy spoke.

"Nothing." Daddy sat down without taking off his coat.

Unable to stand the sad, worried look on his father's face, Chris turned away and got up from the table. "Can I ride my skateboard for a while?"

"Don't be long. We go to your uncle's, you know."

"I won't be long," Chris said and went to get his elbow and knee pads.

The sun was shining brightly, but it did not warm the afternoon. With his helmet securely fastened, Chris pushed off on his way. The cold wind stung his face as he moved against it. He swallowed hard, trying to remove the lump in his throat. But tears he could not hold back smarted on his cheeks. He

**44**

felt stupid, crying. Glad that he had to be aware of every crack and crease in the pavement, of every tree, person, and place he passed, he propelled himself, stopping only for curbs. *Why can't Daddy find a job? He might have to go away again. No, no, not that.*

At a distance he saw Miles and Jamal resting on their bikes, talking to some girls. Chris turned quickly and started home, but not before they had seen him.

They raced after him, shouting his name. He quickly wiped his face with the back of his hand. He braced himself, hoping they would not notice his pain.

"Hey, birthday boy," Jamal shouted. "You were some surprised." Jamal and Miles sat on their bikes while Chris rested on the curb. "You should've seen your face when you came through your uncle's door, man." Jamal bent over with laughter.

"And you almost messed it up, Jamal," Miles scolded.

"When?" Chris asked.

"Remember when we talked about Kwanzaa and he said that was why your uncle had asked us to come to his house on Christmas Day?" Miles answered.

"You looked funny, man. That was good." Jamal couldn't stop laughing.

Chris slipped off his helmet. "You really gonna come to Kwanzaa, huh?"

"I want to. But I don't know if I'll like it, man," Jamal said.

"I like it," Miles responded. "But we don't do it at

**45**

our house. We always go to your uncle's, huh, Chris? And to the community center."

"Yeah. We all go over to my uncle's every year, too. Uncle Ronald's into that kinda stuff."

"You'll like it, Jamal." Miles grinned. "It's fun, huh, Chris?"

"And it's serious, too," Chris said.

"I don't like serious stuff, man," Jamal muttered. "Like school and church."

"Not that kind of serious, huh, Chris?" Miles asked.

"Some of it's fun. You make things and listen to people tell stories. Older people talk about what they remember, stuff like that. I like it, especially the drums and music." Chris's enthusiasm came through.

"My whole family goes," Miles said.

"My family's just me and my mama," Jamal said softly.

"Not at Kwanzaa," Chris said. "Everybody is your family at Kwanzaa, right, Miles?"

"Yeah, that's Kwanzaa. But you have to go to know. We going tonight," Miles said.

Chris put on his helmet and pushed off on his skateboard. Miles and Jamal rode their bikes alongside him near the walk.

"If we come to your uncle's, do we have to get dressed up?" Jamal asked.

"Not unless you want to," Chris answered. "Wear anything you want. Just come, okay?"

"And no giggling at the Swahili words," Miles demanded.

"Aw, you intelligent, huh, Jamal?" Chris asked.

**46**

"I hope so." Jamal gave a little laugh. "I've heard Swahili before. *Habari gani*. That means, What's the news? Like we say, What's happening?"

"All right!" Chris exclaimed. He stepped off his board to slap Jamal's palms. "My uncle starts things on time. You guys don't be late, now."

# EIGHT

That evening Chris's uncle greeted his guests standing by his door in a long white *kanzu*. The living room had a festive air. Black, red, and green balloons floated among paper streamers. The black, red, and green *bendera*, the flag, stood out. Chris, in his colorful *dashiki*, felt a pulse of quiet excitement.

Many of the women had on dresses in African styles. Chris thought that his mother's pale blue *busuti* was especially beautiful. On her head she wore a *gele*, of the same material as her *busuti*. Chris watched as she talked with Jamal's mother, and he felt pleased that she looked so pretty.

Grandma Ida, round and plump, looked regal in a plum-colored high-crowned *gele* the same color as her loosely fitting *buba*. She laughed and talked with the people near her.

**49**

Voices quieted when Uncle Ronald moved toward the center of the room. People took seats in a circle with the table in the middle. The elderly sat closest, with the children on the floor at their feet. Feeling the warm friendliness in the room, Chris smiled at Miles and Jamal. Then he took hold of Beth's hand and waited.

Uncle Ronald's deep, strong voice filled the room. "Welcome to our first day of Kwanzaa celebration. You are going to hear a lot of Swahili tonight."

"Why Swahili?" one of the children whispered.

"It's African. We African-Americans." The response was whispered, also.

"Now," Uncle Ronald went on, "this is the first day of our celebration of togetherness. A time for remembering our past and looking at where we are today. It is a time for us to make promises for a better life for ourselves and for our children. Everybody can take part, especially the young people here.

"Chris, Miles, and Beth, y'all come on up and help me. Some of us here are new and don't know what all these things are on the table."

The table was covered with a cotton cloth tie-dyed in black, green, and red. All the symbols of Kwanzaa were on the table. Chris knew that Uncle Ronald had brought many of those things home from Kenya when he returned from the Peace Corps.

Uncle Ronald continued, "The children will give us the Swahili words for the symbols and tell us what they mean. You will repeat after them so we'll all learn together, okay? Beth, you go first."

On the table were apples, oranges, and bananas in a large, hand-carved wooden bowl, surrounded by

greens, carrots, yams, squash, coconuts, and many ears of corn. "This is *mazao*, which means crops," Beth said. "All the food stands for rewards for our work. Like farmers have to work, watering plants and pulling weeds, we have to work hard for prizes and awards." Beth smiled as everyone applauded.

Miles had a turn defining the *mkeka*, a mat woven from palm leaves. "The mat and fruit bowl came from Africa," he said. "In Africa people make a lot of things by hand. That is an old custom. This *mkeka* stands for our history."

Then Miles explained that the candle holder, or *kinara*, stands for ancestors, parents, and all Black people. "The *kinara* holds the flame," Miles said. "And the corn, the *vibunzi*, stands for children, an ear for each child."

"That was a great job, Miles," Uncle Ronald said. "Let's give Miles a big hand." Everybody applauded.

Chris felt nervous at his turn, but relaxed as he got going. He told about the gaily wrapped gifts on the table. "These *zawadi* stand for all the things children have said they would do and have done. They also represent things parents have done for children."

He placed his hand on a cup made from a gourd. "This is a *kikombe cha umoja*, the unity cup. This cup is used for drinks in honor of our ancestors," Chris said. "The seven candles here in the *kinara* are called *mishumaa saba*. They represent the seven principles of Kwanzaa, what we believe in."

Chris then explained that the colors of the candles also had meaning. "The black one stands for our people, the three green ones on the right are for youth and hope for the future, and the red ones on the left stand for struggle that goes on and on."

Chris got a big hand, too. When he sat down he smiled at Miles and Jamal. His heart beat faster when they smiled back.

"*Habari gani*," Uncle Ronald cried. "*Kwanzaa yenu iwe heri!*"

"*Umoja!*" everyone responded.

The ritual for the first day of Kwanzaa began. Beth lighted the first candle. As she held the match to the black candle in the center of the *kinara*, she said, "We begin this first day of Kwanzaa, *umoja*, which means unity."

Everyone remained quiet as small cups of grape juice were passed around. By the light of the candle, Uncle Ronald poured some juice into the *kikombe*. Then he set a small flowerpot filled with earth on the floor. "This earth is a mixture from Kenya, a West African country in our native land, and from America, our new land." He lifted the cup. "For all of our mothers and fathers unknown to us in our native land of Africa, we make this *tambiko*, or libation." He poured the drink into the pot of earth.

He refilled the cup and lifted it. Chris raised his cup with all the others in the room.

Uncle Ronald then began the *tamshi la tambiko*. "For all of our people known everywhere who struggled for freedom; for our brothers, Malcolm, Martin, and Medgar; for our sisters, Mary Church, Fannie Lou, and Ida B. May they live in the hearts of freedom-loving people as long as the earth turns warmed by the sun." He drank from the cup as all the people in the room drank from theirs.

53

Then people were invited to stand and talk about *umoja* in their lives, or in the lives and history of Black people. Chris listened with interest when one woman talked about Harriet Tubman and how Harriet practiced the unity principle when she helped slaves follow the North Star and run away to freedom. Then his father stood to speak. Chris felt an uneasy surprise.

"So far, all the things talked about tonight have been happenings in the past. I can speak of *umoja* in the present, today," he said. "As most of you know, I'm out of work."

Chris could not look at his father. He felt a heaviness in his chest.

His father went on. "I can say there has been unity in my family and among my friends. You have shared food and other goods. You have given your support and understanding, too. I want to thank all of you. I think I can speak for Myra, a good wife and mother, and for Chris and Beth, too, when I say we are proud to be a part of you. But we might have to leave here...."

Chris, still feeling uneasy, glanced at Mama. She held her head down and Chris sensed that she was close to tears. *Oh, no. Don't let her cry.* The heavy lump in his chest spread as he fought back his tears. He'd just die if Miles and Jamal saw *him* crying.

His father sat down and there was silence. Then Uncle Ronald stood and said, "Come on, everybody. It's time for some food. Time for fun! Let's begin the *karamu.*"

There were baskets of bread, bowls of fruit punch, platters of meat and vegetables, and pans of pies and cobblers. All the children were served first. Then the elderly helped themselves. Chris's mama and daddy and the other people in between served themselves last.

After the feast, some of Uncle Ronald's friends beat drums. Music, dancing, and laughter went on into the night. But in spite of all the good food and entertainment, Chris was glad when the celebration ended. He went home feeling more worried and afraid than ever.

# NINE

The shrill ringing of the telephone brought Chris out of deep sleep. Then he heard his daddy's voice. The search for a job went on. *How do people find work?* he wondered.

"Chris," Daddy called.

Chris hurriedly put on his robe and met his daddy in the hallway. "You got a job?" His voice cracked with excitement.

"Well, something. You take over until your mama comes, okay?"

If Daddy had a job, why didn't he look happy? Chris wanted to ask some questions. But he decided not to.

"Oh," Daddy said. "I almost forgot. This is where I'll be." Chris took the small piece of paper and looked at it. "The phone number is there, but you're not to call ..."

"...unless there's an emergency," Chris finished the sentence. They both laughed.

As he followed his daddy through the house toward the garage, Chris noticed a neatly wrapped package on the table. "What's that?" he asked.

"Your uncle brought that for Kwanzaa. Yours and Beth's. Don't open it now. Not until Beth is up," Daddy said. "Bye now."

Alone, Chris toyed with the ribbons. Tempted, he pulled the attached cluster of ribbons off the top. *Beth won't know the difference*, he thought. Then he decided to get her up. He stuck the ribbon back in place.

He didn't have to get Beth up. Right then she stumbled into the room like someone walking in her sleep. But when she saw the package, she became wide awake. "We got a present," she cried.

They wasted no time unwrapping the box. Inside were three things: a magic slate for Beth, a booklet neatly done in Uncle Ronald's handwriting, and a small *kinara* with the black, green, and red *mishumaa saba*.

"Let's light the candles," Beth said.

"No. We have to wait until Mama and Daddy get home. We'll do it together." He began to read a note he had found with the booklet.

Dear Chris,
This *kinara* is for you to use to observe the remaining six days and principles of Kwanzaa listed for you in this booklet. Each day, light a candle. Then remind your family of the principle for that day and for what that principle stands. We have celebrated *umoja*. Today, you will cel-

ebrate *kujichagulia*, which means self-determination.

The other five principles are: *ujima*, collective
work and responsibility; *ujamaa*, cooperative
economics; *nia*, purpose; *kuumba*, creativity;
and *imani*, faith.


"What you reading?" Beth wanted to know. "What
does it say?"

"It's for me. Uncle Ronald is putting me in charge.
I'll do the Kwanzaa for us this year." He looked at
her and grinned proudly.

"But what does it say?" she persisted.

Chris continued reading aloud: "'All of this may
seem hard at first...'" He stopped and looked at
Beth. "The principles of Kwanzaa, you know."

"Yeah. Like *umoja*," she said.

Chris read on: "'But you will learn all the seven
principles—the *nguzo*—and when you're older,
you'll understand exactly what they mean.'"

He looked at Beth and knew she was not listening.
She was scribbling letters and numbers on her magic
slate.

Chris wondered what Miles and Jamal were doing.
They're probably together right now, he thought. If
only Mama would let them come over when he had
to stay in to take care of Beth.

Beth opened the blinds and shouted, "Ooo, look!"

Chris joined her at the window. Snow falling thick
and fast blanketed the walk and street. Wind pushed
and shoved the silent snow hurling down, sticking,
growing. Steam flowed from vents and dark smoke
curled from chimneys, white against the lead-colored

59

sky. A lone car moved cautiously in the street, its wheels making a muffled sluicing. Chris sensed an inner hum in the silence. A peaceful satisfaction.

All too soon he was brought back to the present with Beth's cry, "I'm hungry. Let's eat."

Reluctantly he moved with her toward the kitchen, wishing he could go back to bed.

By the time Mama came home, he and Beth had tired of one another. Breakfast, lunch, a little talk, reading aloud, and lots of unanswerable questions from a five-year-old left him feeling restless and bored.

He greeted Mama with the news that Daddy had found a job. *Was it a good job?* he wondered now. *Or just a few days of work?* He didn't want the family to have to move.

Mama was pleased to hear about the job. Things were different at home when she was happy. Soon the house had an aroma of corn bread cooking and meat and vegetables warming. Her good feelings spread to Chris and Beth. They set the table, laughing and teasing as they put the small *kinara* on the buffet and placed fruit festively around it. Beth stuck the matches under the edge of her plate, claiming the right to light the candle.

When Daddy came home they all rushed to him. "How is the new job?" Mama asked.

"I don't want to talk about it." Daddy walked through to the bedroom and closed the door.

In silence they put food on the table. Soon the family was seated for dinner. Daddy looked tense, tired. Chris announced that he and Beth would do

60

the Kwanzaa ritual. With the booklet turned to pages about the second day, he asked Beth if she was ready. She nodded and came to stand on the other side of the *kinara*.

Chris felt the uneasiness that had begun when Daddy arrived. At first he didn't know how to begin. Then, remembering his uncle's approach, he stood tall and straightened his shoulders. *"Habari gani!"*

*"Kujichagulia!"* they all responded.

Beth relit the black candle for *umoja*, then lighted a red one. "For *kujichagulia*, the second day of Kwanzaa," she said.

Chris saw a smile spread over his father's face and gathered courage to go on. He read the principle of *kujichagulia*. "Self-determination is deciding things, speaking up for ourselves, and doing things the way we feel they should be done."

In the glow of the candles they ate. Chris still felt underlying tension and knew why Mama cautiously chose words, trying to prevent silence from settling around them. Unpleasant things were not allowed to surface at the table while they were eating.

"Well, Bruce, do you want to tell us about the job now?" Mama asked as soon as they had finished dinner.

"There is no job." Daddy spoke with some sharpness. "It was a day's work with little pay."

"What was it?" Chris asked timidly.

"I don't want to talk about it."

"Why? Why can't you talk about it?" Mama was less cautious.

"I'm getting tired of going on these little penny-paying jobs thinking they're going to turn into something and it's always the same—nothing."

There was silence. Chris didn't remember ever hearing such bitterness in his daddy's voice. He kept his eyes on his plate as Daddy went on. "I feel like giving up and never going out there again."

"Now certainly is not the time to think of giving up," Mama said.

"You think I'm not even trying. I know you think I'm no longer the man of this house with you taking care of us," Daddy said angrily.

"How can you say that?" She tried to take the edge off of his anger. "That's not what I think at all, Bruce. I still think there is something out there for you."

"I'm glad you think so. There may be jobs, but not for me. I file an application and I'm told I'm over-qualified. If I get to an interview, one look at me and I'm just not what they're looking for."

*One look at me* rang in Chris's mind. *This is happening because we're Black.*

"You'll find something." Mama sounded as if she were pleading for Daddy to hang in there.

"I've found nothing all this time. I'm beginning to think I'll never find anything again. I can't go on like this."

Chris looked up and caught Mama's eye. She turned to Daddy and said, "I wish you wouldn't talk like this in front of the children."

"I said I didn't want to talk about it. You insisted. They need to know the truth. A man can't determine what he's going to do with his life if he has no job." He left the table, put on his coat, and said, "I'll be back."

They waited and waited. Beth and Mama went to

bed. Chris waited some more. Finally he went to his room. He lay in his bed. *What is Daddy doing out there in the cold night? What will happen to us if he never comes back?* He tried to recall the feeling he'd had while looking at the snow that morning. The sleep he had longed for then would not come now. Every sound alerted him. Not until he heard the car in the driveway and the door to his parents' bedroom close did he fall asleep.

# TEN

Another day went by; the weather warmed. Sun and snow made the sky unbelievably blue. The city sparkled, but Chris's mood did not reflect the change. With Beth taking a nap, bored, he paced from room to room, restless. *The holiday almost gone and I've had no fun. Stuck in this house with Beth, can't even see my friends.*

The night before, they had lighted the candle for *ujima*, collective work and responsibility. The worried look on Mama's face had kept him from saying much about *ujima*. Now, Chris felt ashamed of his restlessness. He knew he was with Beth because they had no money for the sitter. He wanted to be cooperative, responsible. He could really help if he had a bicycle, but that couldn't even be mentioned without a hassle.

Later, he and Beth had just popped some corn

when the doorbell rang. Beth ran ahead of him to the door.

"Wait," he said. "Let me see who's there."

"It's me. Your favorite uncle," said a voice from outside.

Laughing, they opened the door to let Uncle Ronald in.

"That popcorn sure smells good."

"Come on, you can have some," Beth said.

"Later. I came to celebrate *ujamaa* with you guys. Let's do the ritual and you can do it again with your mom and dad tonight."

Beth and Chris took turns relighting the three candles. Then Beth lighted a red one, the fourth, for *ujamaa*.

"Cooperative economics," Uncle Ronald said. "That principle has to do with making money by working together."

Chris thought about Daddy and said nothing.

"Mama makes the money in this house now," Beth said.

"Aw, shut up," Chris muttered angrily.

"Let her talk, Chris. Your mama does make money. Your daddy, too. He'll be working steadily again, soon. But I was thinking we should start a business. Work for ourselves. Wait a minute."

Uncle Ronald went out and came back into the house rolling a red bicycle with streaks of black and green. A streamlined one.

"Uncle Ronald!" Chris screamed. "Is that for me?"

"For *ujamaa*. All of us, everybody in our family, got together and bought you this bicycle. That's one

**66**

means of cooperative economics. You can start your paper route business."

"Oh, I can't believe this," Chris cried. "How'd you know I wanted to deliver papers?"

"Your mama told me."

"Now I can deliver them."

"While Beth and I find something to do, why don't you go out and visit your friends?" Uncle Ronald suggested.

Trembling with joy, Chris booted the kickstand, making sure it was in place. He wheeled the bike out to the sidewalk. Then, swinging his leg over the top tube, he pumped down and broke free. He raced away, not noticing the coldest wind, everything whirring by, blurred. He felt weightless. There was only one thing in his mind: *It's mine, it's mine*, he said over and over to himself.

Miles came out of his back door just as Chris rode into his open garage and braked his bike.

"I saw you coming," Miles said. "Is that yours?"

"It's mine. Got it for *ujamaa*, cooperative economics day."

"All right!" Miles smiled.

"Now I can deliver papers, too." Chris breathed hard with excitement.

"You're just in time. I'm waiting for Mr. Moore right now. He's bringing my papers. He's the district manager."

"Think he'll hire me?"

"He might. Wait and ask him."

Soon a truck loaded with newspapers drove up. A stocky man jumped out and grabbed a stack of papers. "I can always depend on you, Miles," he said, dropping the bundle.

Miles introduced Chris to Mr. Moore and told him Chris wanted to deliver papers.

"What kind of work is your dad doing?" Mr. Moore asked.

"He's not working now," Chris said with his head lowered.

"Oh, too bad. You need somebody with a steady job to vouch for you. You know, back you up. You have to be responsible."

"Oh, Chris is responsible," Miles said.

Chris looked at Mr. Moore and said eagerly, "And my mama works. She's a nurse. And my uncle. They'll vouch for me."

"You'll have to be bonded," Mr. Moore said. "That's a kind of insurance."

"How much a bond cost?" Chris asked.

"Three hundred dollars."

"Three hundred dollars!" Chris screamed.

"Oh, don't get excited now." Mr. Moore laughed. "You'll have to pay it, but not all at once. Now, if you were eighteen or older, you'd have to pay it before you went to work."

"I paid mine a little at a time, till I paid it all, huh, Mr. Moore?" Miles said.

"Yeah. That's right. Only grown-ups have to pay up front."

"Whew!" Chris shook his head rapidly. "Then you'll hire me?"

"I guess I can use a boy like you. You ten?"

"Just made eleven, huh, Miles?" Chris beamed.

"Fine. You can start in right after the holiday."

69

Mr. Moore straightened papers around in his truck. He turned to Chris. "Oh, yeah, I won't be your manager. Somebody else will train you."

"How come you won't do it, Mr. Moore?" Miles wanted to know.

"Miles, didn't I tell you? I got promoted. I thought I had told you I'm going to be a supervisor." Mr. Moore grinned and went on his way.

"He's real nice," Miles said. "Wish he wasn't leaving."

Suddenly Chris had an idea. "You think my dad could get *his* job?"

"Sure," Miles answered excitedly, "if he's got three hundred dollars."

*You don't have to come up with that kind of money. Only grown-ups do,* flashed into Chris's mind. *Where will we get three hundred dollars right away?*

Chris rode home worried. He had thought getting a bicycle and a job delivering papers would make him the happiest person in the world. But instead, he was more anxious than ever about his father getting a job.

That night he tossed and turned. He hadn't told his family about Mr. Moore and the jobs. How could Mama and Uncle Ronald get three hundred dollars for Daddy? *My bike. I could give it back. That would bring some money. Maybe two hundred dollars. Oh no, never. Not that. I want my bike.* He tossed and turned some more, and finally fell into troubled sleep.

The next morning Chris woke feeling tired. He couldn't figure out a way to tell his parents about the job openings without offering to give up his bike.

70

All day he moped around, irritable. He was short-tempered with Beth. Though the weather had warmed even more and the sun shone brightly, he refused to let her go outside. He wouldn't even let her open the blinds.

"You're a mean brother," Beth accused him with tears in her voice.

Chris moved restlessly about the sunless rooms, feeling miserable. Why was he being so mean? He didn't want to be. He wanted to go find Beth, open the blinds, and play with her outside. But he just couldn't bring himself to do it.

His parents came home together that evening. When Beth saw them she burst into tears, trying to tell them how mean Chris had been.

Chris stood under their glares wishing they could understand what he was feeling.

"It's all right, Beth," Mama said. "We're home now, and guess what? Daddy and I brought us all some pizza for supper. Come on. Wanta help me get it ready?"

Chris and his father sat together, waiting, in that dreadful silence that had crept into their house and that no one seemed able to shatter. The quiet increased Chris's uneasiness. *Why doesn't Daddy say something? Why doesn't he wanta know why I've been so mean? Say something! Anything, but something.*

Before eating, Chris lit the candle for *nia*, the fifth principle, which stresses purpose. He had a purpose: to deliver papers and help his family. But he didn't want to talk about that.

They ate pizza and salad by candlelight. He could tell that Beth had a hand in the salad. It was loaded

**71**

with sunflower seeds. Even though it was a delicious supper, no one savored the food. The meal ended quickly.

"May I be excused?" Chris asked, getting up from the table.

"In just a minute," Daddy said.

Chris sat down, sensing something important about to happen. Maybe Daddy had found a job at last. *But that should make them happy*. He waited. Nothing but that awful silence.

Finally Daddy spoke softly. "Well, your mama and I have decided that we will have to leave this place."

"You mean move to another town?" Chris cried.

"Yes." Mama did not look up.

"Oh, no, I can't leave here. Not now. What about Grandma Ida, Uncle Ronald, the family?"

"Why do you always have to think of just yourself?" Mama scolded.

Chris felt stung. He looked at Daddy, pained.

"She didn't mean it the way it sounds, son. She's trying to tell you we're all hurting. It's our family, too, you know."

"But you can find work here," Chris cried.

"Now, Chris, I've looked. You know that. Every single day for almost two years."

Feeling desperate, Chris blurted out, "There is a job. At the newspaper. A manager's job." He told what he knew about Mr. Moore's promotion. He wanted to tell them about his job, too. But he thought about the bond for him and his daddy, six hundred dollars. He would surely have to give up the bicycle. He decided not to mention his own job at all.

# ELEVEN

On the morning of New Year's Eve, Chris's house crackled with excitement and anticipation. Mama had a day off, and Daddy had an appointment with Mr. Moore to see about the job. The appointment was for that afternoon. Even though it was New Year's Eve, the job had to be filled right away.

"How would you and Beth like to get out of the house to do something today?" Mama asked.

Chris, still worried about the bond money, was not sure. He only wanted to stay in his room away from everybody and everything. "Like what?"

"Like going to the community center. A lot of your friends will be there doing creative things today." Today was the sixth day of Kwanzaa, *kuumba*, based on the principle of creativity.

"I wanta go." Beth liked the idea.

"I don't know," Chris said.

"Chris, you need to get out of this house. I want you to go," Mama pleaded.

"Well, all right. I'll go."

Mama dropped them off at the center just in time for the lighting of the sixth candle. Miles and Jamal were there, happy to see Chris.

"We know you're going to woodwork," Jamal announced to Chris.

"Yeah. Where y'all going?"

"I'm going to essay writing," Miles said.

"I'm going to poetry," Jamal said.

"You, poetry? I don't believe it," Chris said.

"Me," Jamal said, beating his chest. "Believe it. I'm gonna surprise you."

"Well, I can hardly wait. Roses are red, violets, blue . . ." Chris laughed.

"I'll laugh last, man, what you bet?" Jamal bragged.

Chris took Beth to the paper arts section and hurried to woodwork. He had decided to make a big *kinara* for his family to have for next year's Kwanzaa. He explained to the instructor, Mr. Pierce, that he wanted the *kinara* in the shape of the African continent. Immediately they got busy drawing the design: three candle holders on the east side of Africa, three on the west, and one at the southern tip.

He watched as the wood took shape under the zing of the electric saw. Soon he had sanded and smoothed the form and painted it black.

"What you using for candle holders on that wood?" Mr. Pierce asked.

"You think it'll burn, huh?"

74

"Not likely, but I'd make sure."

Chris had been thinking about making this *kinara* for a long time. Why hadn't he thought of safe holders? *The holders should be metal!*

Looking around the place, he finally found what he needed: a long, thin strip of tin. While measuring the tin he hit upon an idea for a special design. With a hammer and small nail, he pounded little holes all over the tin. As he worked, his mind wandered to his daddy. *What if he gets that job? I'll have to give up my bicycle for his bond. I don't wanta give it up. If only we weren't Black.*

His thoughts flashed to his family, to Uncle Ronald, and he felt ashamed and guilty. *What would Uncle Ronald say if he knew I wished we weren't Black?* He pushed that painful thought out of his mind by pounding the tin harder.

Time seemed to fly, and Chris wondered if he'd have time to finish before Mama came to take them home. He carefully used the heavy scissors to cut seven pieces of tin four inches long. Then he clipped each around the bottom and folded it, making holders that could be glued upright on the board.

"Gosh, it's not dry," he said aloud to the room. He waited. Again his mind wandered to Daddy. Trying to forget that, he focused on the noise about him. People hammered and sawed. From the other rooms came the sound of music and feet moving in dance.

He decided to make gifts for Miles and Jamal while he waited. He drew profiles of Malcolm X and Martin Luther King on pieces of wood. When Mr. Pierce had cut them on the saw, Chris sanded them and painted them with black watercolor. That would dry fast.

**75**

Finally the form was dry and ready for the candle holders. The silver color on the black wood looked amazingly attractive. The pounding had created raised designs of small people, birds, and animals. Mr. Pierce invited the other people working in the shop to stop and look at the *kinara*. Chris felt pride and satisfaction.

When Chris and Beth came outside looking for Mama, Miles and Jamal were waiting. The three friends exchanged gifts with a promise not to open them until they got home. Miles and Jamal took off on their bikes.

Soon Mama came. Before getting into the car, Chris cried, "Did Daddy get the job?"

"I don't know yet. I've been so busy. Your grandma called. The family wants to celebrate the New Year at our house. We're going to have a party."

"Can I come?" Beth cried.

"Can't you hear? It's at our house, silly," Chris told her. "Anyway, you'll probably be asleep before it starts."

"Aw, Chris, please," Mama scolded. "Sure, Beth, you can come."

Chris sighed and sank back into the seat. Since he had first heard about the jobs and bonds he had not had a moment of peace. "You know, Mama, I don't think Daddy'll git that job."

"Why you say a thing like that?"

"He'll need three hundred dollars." Chris then told her about his job. "I'll have to pay three hundred dollars, too, but I can pay mine out of what I earn delivering papers. We don't have that kind of money, do we?"

76

"No, we don't."

"I could take my bike back."

"You don't like your bike?" Beth asked.

"Yeah, but..."

"You will not give up your bike," said Mama. "No, no indeed, Chris. That's awfully nice of you to offer, but you are not responsible for getting your daddy a job. Your daddy and I will handle that."

"But you don't have the money. You didn't have any for Christmas and my birthday."

Mama gave a little laugh. "That's different, Chris. Of course we wouldn't borrow money for gifts, but for a job we would. Please don't worry."

Chris did worry. He could hardly wait to get home to see if things had gone well for Daddy.

Daddy was not there when they arrived. Grandma Ida, Uncle Ronald, and the aunts were there, and the house was full of hustle and bustle. *Daddy's got to get that job. We can't leave our family. Where will we go?* He hurried to his room and closed the door.

He sat on his bed and tried to control the fear. Noise and laughter resounded throughout the house. Chris didn't want to feel so all alone. He hurried from his room.

Uncle Ronald had everything ready for the last ritual of Kwanzaa. There was a delicious aroma of food cooking, and Grandma Ida's voice rang from the kitchen. "What's New Year's without black-eyed peas and collard greens? Peas for good luck and collards for the greenback all year long! No house should be without them on New Year's Day."

"Cook, Mama," one of Chris's aunts said. "We need some luck, *and* we sure need some greenback."

"What's greenback, Grandma?" Beth wanted to know.

"Money, honey," Grandma exclaimed. Everybody laughed.

Chris listened to the laughter and fun and some of his sadness disappeared. But why didn't Daddy come home?

It was now almost ten o'clock. People were coming in and out, but still Daddy hadn't come. Chris finally asked, "Where's Daddy?"

"He'll be here," Mama said. "Stop worrying, Chris. C'mon, have some fun."

"Yeah," Grandma Ida put in. "We don't like long faces in this family. I'm getting old, and you're gonna have to take my place, Chris, keeping the laughter alive. Don't ever forget how to laugh, boy."

That kind of talk made Chris even more sad. He wandered back to his room and decided to open his gifts from Miles and Jamal. Miles had prepared a booklet on three African-American scientists. Chris glanced through paragraphs about a famous biologist, Ernest E. Just. He had heard about George Washington Carver and Charles Drew, but never of Ernest E. Just.

When he opened Jamal's gift, he smiled. There was the promised poem.

> Drums! Drums! Drumming!
> To the beat moving feet
> Making tracks, shaping roads
> In the drumming voices humming
> Your turn, your turn, your turn.

Chris read the poem thinking about what his grandma had said about laughing. *And maybe it's my turn to stop worrying so much. Even if I have to give my bike up, I'll give it up!* He read Jamal's poem again. "All right!" he said aloud to the room. "I'll give you the last laugh!"

Just then Chris heard the sound of the car in the driveway. Daddy was home. He ran to the front of the house. The pleased look on his father's face let Chris know that he had the job.

"What kept you so long?" Mama asked.

"I had to see the territory. Mr. Moore took me around tonight." He turned to Chris. "Why didn't you tell me? I was surprised to learn that my very own son will be my first trainee." He grabbed Chris and hugged him.

"But what about the bond?" Chris asked worriedly.

"Mr. Moore was very impressed. He said you let him know right away that our family is behind you."

"No. *Your* bond," Mama said.

"District managers don't put up bonds. Only the carriers do that," Daddy answered.

"What?" Chris cried. "After all of that! And I thought I'd have to...whew!" Relieved, Chris was ready to get on with the party. When twelve o'clock arrived he joined in blowing whistles, tossing streamers, and hugging and kissing everybody to bring in the New Year.

Right after midnight, they woke Beth to join them for the last ritual of Kwanzaa. Chris relit the six candles and Beth, still not wide awake, said, "I light the seventh candle for *imani*, the principle of faith."

After drinking *tambiko* from the *kikombe cha*

*umoja*, Grandma Ida talked about faith. "Black people through ups and downs have practiced *imani*. When our rights were denied, we kept the faith. When we were bitten by dogs and bombed with water, we kept the faith. And as a family we practice *imani*. We keep the faith. We stand together, and tonight we celebrate that unity and faith without fear that Bruce, Myra, Chris, and Beth will be separated from us. So come, let's rejoice."

They celebrated with a feast of black-eyed peas and rice, mustard and collard greens, yams, okra, and much more, by the light of seven candles. When they opened their gifts for the end of Kwanzaa and the beginning of the New Year, Chris had a great surprise. Grandma Ida gave him a seat bag for his bicycle that she had made with her very own hands.

Chris presented his *kinara* to his parents. "I made this for our family so we can celebrate Kwanzaa in our house every year from now on." They all touched the *kinara*, amazed at its beauty.

"That boy is sure good with his hands," Grandma Ida said.

"Yes, he is," Mama agreed. "But he's not only clever with his hands, he has a big heart, too."

Chris knew she was talking about his offer to give up his bicycle. He beamed with pride. *Maybe Uncle Ronald was right, after all, when he said that important people give.*

In the wee hours of the morning, the family made a circle around Grandma Ida, Beth, and Chris. Grandma Ida gave the *tamshi la tutaonana* : "In this new year let us continue to practice *umoja, kujichagulia, ujima, ujamaa, nia, kuumba*, and *imani*. Let

**81**

us strive to do something that will last as long as the earth turns and water flows."

"Now," Uncle Ronald said, "let's leave this house with the word *harambee*. In Swahili that means pulling together."

"*Harambee!*" they all shouted. They repeated it seven times, with Chris's voice the loudest of them all.

# SWAHILI GLOSSARY

Swahili vowels are pronounced as follows:

a = like the *a* in car
e = like the *a* in play
i = like the *ee* in fee
o = like the *oe* in toe
u = like the *oo* in moo

The consonants are pronounced the same as they are in the English language. The *g* in *gele* is hard, like the *g* in go. The accent is almost always on the next-to-last syllable in the words used here.

*harambee* (ha-ram-be), a call to unity and collective struggle, pulling together.

*karamu* (ka-ra-mu), feast.

*kwanza* (kwan-za), first.

*Kwanzaa* (kwan-za), an African-American holiday celebration that begins on December 26 and ends January 1. Founded in 1966 by Dr. Maulana Karenga, the holiday is a time of ingathering of African-Americans to celebrate their history.

*nguzo* (n-gu-zo), principles.

*saba* (sa-ba), seven.

*tambiko* (tam-bi-ko), pouring drink for ancestors—a libation.

*tamshi la tambiko* (tam-shi la tam-bi-ko), statement made when pouring drink for ancestors.

*tamshi la tutaonana* (tam-shi la tu-ta-o-na-na), statement of farewell.


## SEVEN PRINCIPLES OF KWANZAA

*imani* (i-ma-ni), faith.

*kujichagulia* (ku-ji-cha-gu-lia), self-determination.

*kuumba* (ku-um-ba), creativity.

*nia* (ni-a), purpose.

*ujamaa* (u-ja-ma), cooperative economics.

*ujima* (u-ji-ma), collective work and responsibility.

*umoja* (u-mo-ja), unity.


## RITUAL SYMBOLS OF KWANZAA

*bendera* (ben-de-ra), flag.

*kikombe* (ki-kom-be), a cup.

*kikombe cha umoja* (ki-kom-be cha u-mo-ja), unity cup.

*kinara* (ki-na-ra), candle holder.

*mazao* (ma-za-o), crops.

*mkeka* (m-ke-ka), mat.

*mishumaa* (mi-shu-ma-a), candles.

*mishumaa saba* (mi-shu-ma-a sa-ba), seven candles.

*vibunzi* (vi-bun-zi), ears of corn.
*zawadi* (za-wa-di), gift or gifts.

## SWAHILI GREETINGS

*Habari gani* (ha-ba-ri ga-ni), What's the news?
*Kwanzaa yenu iwe heri* (kwan-za ye-nu i-we he-ri),
   Happy Kwanzaa.

## CLOTHING

*buba* (bu-ba), elegant robe or gown.
*busuti* (bu-su-ti), a robe with a scarf at the waist.
*dashiki* (da-shi-ki), a loosely fitting shirt for boys and
   men; a loosely fitting blouse for girls or women.
*gele* (ge-le), a head wrap.
*kanzu* (kan-zu), a robe for men.